Blues for the Babes

Blues for the Babes

Copyright ©2021 by Marsalis

Blues for the Babes

by

Marsalis

Contents

Blues for the Babes

1

Edison Avenue

Once upon a time in the year ninety-nine
When shit was fine, Caesar-cuts with the line
Fits were Gap Kids, Hype Williams vids
We were still good, not yet on the skids
Parties were at Zap Zone, mind's blown
Dairy Queen dipped cones, Nokia cell phones
Eyes glued tight to the aughties' first hours
Until we saw planes crash through two towers
So came war and terror, no trial and error
Just called the boys, gave 'em toys, sent them out to destroy
a veiled rival, said it's vital for the world's survival
to break the spinal of those adoring the wrong idol
But while the deserts went blast, my parents split fast
Mom left as I drowned darkness in my Dreamcast
In a week's time, I dragged on my first cig
Felt real big, no sprig, explodin like a rig, ya dig?

School was uncool, so we played them like fools
Skippin class, kiss my ass, wanna bake by the pool
Strippin down to our skin, dabbles in the deep-end
When the supply ran dry, we'd call a plug or a friend
For the dro and indo we stayed on the hunt
Once snatched in a batch we'd roll up the blunts
Head down in the Hummer to the college kid bashes
Crash in with our grins and do lines through our lashes
In striped 'Crombie polos and red Solos
We spilled beer and cheap rum on posh Manolos
Gulped down an Addarall, a couple triple c's
When the shit starts to hit, it's like I am the breeze
Soon we dip, for a trip, to cop a bag of shrooms
And if I take them now, I'll probably meet my doom
But shit, man, fuck it, no time for sorrow
We're just gonna do it all again tomorrow

Remember when we danced on the tables in the bar?
Remember when we crashed your daddy's new car?
So young and dumb and full of cum
Nowhere to hide and nowhere to run
But Mom and Dad, they went mad
Told me that they wasn't fuckin wit nunna that
Reminded me of my name and where I came
Told me I was stupid-reckless and should be ashamed
But what did I care? Fuck what was fair!
They fucked up the family, brought on this despair
But my escapes were my mistakes, as it all came down
Joyriding in Jeeps switched to crashing in crowns
Backyard fights became sights for manslaughter
Skinny-dipping turned to bodies floatin in the water
To fight my urge, I had to purge, grabbed my shit, had to pack
Staring down Edison Avenue, I knew I wasn't coming back

2

Cuffing Season

Against common sense, full of great suspense,
I downloaded an app that was nothing but dense
Quickly I regretted, felt fretted, by the desperation
No chill, no respect, no effort, no hesitation
Just "send me pics" and "send me nudes"
"Come on, rush rush, don't be a prude"
"Sit on my face, let me ride, fuck me raw then come inside"
"Let me see it, I know it's thick, I know it's nice, I know it's wide"
And gee, what a dream under other circumstances!
Such easy advances should make you go pant-less!
All the ass and dick and tits thrown your way
should make you thank the Lord you live in this day
But the more pics they share, the less I care
The more skin I see, the less it means
But this app I won't delete, not just yet at least
Must be someone out there who's not such a beast

So I accepted fate, set up some dates
Realized, through these tries, I might find a mate
Could be him, could be her, whatever I prefer
Whatever happens, happens, whatever occurs, occurs
But from the start, in my heart, hit hundreds of darts
My hope was for dopes, it wasn't in the charts
All the games and jokes and puzzles and pokes
made me wanna grab my neck and commence to choke
There was the girl who read texts but never texted back
There was the dude who begged to be whipped in his sack
There was the chick who looked shit like her profile pic
There was the guy who in the eyes would murder you quick
There was the one, in the sun, who brought their partner along
There was the one, with a son, who kept singing old songs
But none were aware, of my scares and blank stares,
kept concocting their chaos as if I wasn't even there

Was it the same in the old days, the same haze?
The same craze, same praise, same malaise?
But not then, couldn't been—no—not that deal
Back then, my friends, we knew how to feel
We knew how to touch, we knew how to wait
We knew how to speak, and how to relate
We knew how to love, not only for the glove
I pray for those ways to the heavens above
But while in this hell, I might as well
mess around, get my jollies in a nutshell
Meet you at the motel, ring the doorbell
Our first caress is like a death knell
to a life of emotions I no longer desire
Throw my pain, let it rain, upon the funeral pyre
And once you crash, I will dash, gone-fierce in a flash
Cuffing season came and went, I didn't bat an eyelash

3

Me and My Weed Man

It started when my old plug got a new phone
Got your digits from a cat close to the hipbone
Said you was it, was legit, took a second to call
Within fifteen minutes, we were meetin at the mall
The loud was proud and you let me have a sample
My eyes went wide and my purity was trampled
Your laughter and your smile put me in a chill mood
And when you rolled another, I knew you'd be my new dude
It was smooth, for a while, just hit you up when I'm out
You'd always text right back, never did I once doubt
You was loyal, such a foil, to the previous one
Used to chase them for hours just for a shotgun
But with you, it was true, you came through every time
Packed fat jumbo bags, even more than I'd buy
And then that night, we felt right, and you leaned to my face
Then we kissed, such a bliss, gee, my heart was a-race

Before too long I was coming for the ride
Transportin dro with you to the West Side
Bobbin with your bros, hangin with your homies
I always wondered if they knew that you blow me
But your mystery was honestly part of the allure
Whatever you wanted, I was never quite sure
On the Jefferson, I'd watch your puckish grin
Your smooth skin tastin like the sweetest sin
At the casino, we'd gamble shit for kicks
Takin shots at the slots, between rubs and licks
Didn't care what eyes stared, it was do or dare
Then we'd head to the car and continue it there
You cruise the boulevard, I see you gettin hard
Before we hit the strip joint, I catch you off-guard
Lookin up at you, I have your future in my hands
The best in the land, me and my weed man

The more you grew bolder, I watched your shoulder
Those reds and blues flashin, had my heart dashin
But you said not to worry, don't be scurry
That I was paranoid, my vision's gettin blurry
Started askin me to chill back, stay home
And if you wanted to hang, you'd come roam
But I knew it was someone else, not just me
You had another girlfriend and a little baby
Only three, and you didn't wanna mix the two
You had more important shit to do
Like rob a crew or get a new tattoo
The same shit excuse, all this déjà vu
And I know we were through, on that last liquor run
You kept lookin at the rearview, your eyes outdone
Then they came for you, baby, it was part of the plan
Your arrest, killed my chest, me and my weed man

4

Scammer's Saga

The old lady left me for another baby
But I got her AmEx Gold and Visa on hold
Gonna pay off this phone and go on a spree
Get some new shit, you comin with me?

Fuck yes, just look at how I'm dressed
Bum from below, lookin ass from the chest
Need some new sneaks, new tees, a new vest
I want it all, everything, everything in excess

Yessir, I concur, we're singin the same song
I've been in these jogs and jeans for too long
Need a new change, need a new wardrobe
If I don't get it soon, I'm gonna fuckin explode

Now, hold on chill, bro, remember that lame?
My old flame? Who left the keys to the Range?
Let's hop in and go strange, get deranged
Ball out like we own every stock exchange

So what we gonna seize? The Margielas and Marnis?
The Guccis, Fendis, a bit of Riccardo Tisci?
I'm ready, muthafucka, to have some fun
Pluck the Prada and pass over the Münn

And Rick Owens too, Raf Simons, Guess? denim up the wahzoo
Off-White totes, Diesel coats, boots from cashmere goats
Ottolinger on my finger, Louis blocks my stares
Keep that Gabbanna, but give me Hood By Air

I'm feelin mean, give me all of your Lee McQueen
All your Supreme, Balmain, and Givenchy
That vintage Kani, cuz you know the score
And if I'm gettin Hermès, then I must get Dior

Oh word, you can hang? With that Valentino and that Golfwang?
That MSFTSrep, Lauren prep, Versace pep, all on deck
Venetta is betta but don't be scary with Burberry
And if I'm goin to hell, I might as well wear Chanel

Okay, but how we gonna cop it all?
You know these wack cards can't cover that sprawl
We need an angle, an idea, a new sham
One we haven't yet done, some kinda true scam

Oh my god, call the squad, hit up the quad
We about to pull another delectable fraud
Bank accounts, porn amounts, hack their Mac
Forgeries, lotteries, charities, in the black

I wouldn't even mind goin on an app
Pickin up an old dude and nuzzle in his lap
Slip him some jackpot, tie him up in knots
Then take a spin in the new yacht that he bought

Got a pyramid and ponzi floatin in my mind
Cuz I don't have no time for a 9-to-5 grind
Just want what I want and want it right now
Don't care how I get it, someway, somehow

5

Looking-Glass

I am nothing when I squint at the screen
Wiping my tears with tissues unclean
The faces glance back in perfection and glow
Such happiness has me feeling so low
If only I could be the same as they are
White smiles, dope style, a true superstar
Living in condos next door to the beach
New cars, cool bars, always in reach
And all of those followers!—all of those fans!
To never once be invisible again!
To have that love and passion and shine!
To sell new products as if they were mine!
But, fuck, what a fantasy to have such fun
To be an influencer is my dream number one
And if I can help it, so be it I will
Whether lie, cheat, beg, borrow, or kill

I am something when I log on the Tok
My videos liked and viewed 'round the clock
All I did was post a clip of a dance
A routine my cousin taught me by chance
And soon they came in droves and swarms
Commenting frantic, I'd created a storm
Soon others posted them doing the same
Then someone gave it an actual name
They called it "The Su Su" as it broke the net
The biggest trending topic, the hottest thing yet
No time to waste, I chased their fascination
Chased their curiosity, chased their adoration
Within a couple weeks, another video surged
This time dancing to a single on the verge
Within a couple hours, the copycats emerged
So happy I could die, you could've written me a dirge

I am everything when I walk in the Con
Smiling at the peons as they whistle and fawn
Giggling to myself of how foolish they appear
Flailing toward my body as if mutilated deer
But they are my subjects and I am so proud
of the way they appear in incredible crowds
Whenever I whistle, they show up in a snap
Their cameras flashing, my own private paps
For it's them who with I've stricken a chord
It's their cash which has let me afford
my brand-new condo and car by the sea
where I can be gorgeous, beautiful, free
And as they scream my name with delight
Nearly sending my body in shivers of fright
I must admit it's greener, this grass
To be on this side of the looking-glass

6

Telegraph Rd.

Whenever the television steals my soul
Whenever the apps take their ruinous toll
Whenever I've burned out my last bowl
I head on Telegraph Rd for a stroll
My Caddie, my baddie, a trustworthy girl
Together we ride through the concrete world
Roaring at red lights prepared for the race
Shining in blackness, the vision of grace
The road it waits for our devious worse
Majestic, enormous, a divine traverse
spreading across all towns and cities
sliding sweetly between the glam and gritty
On Telegraph we began our rousing quest
The sun as our guidance, we truly felt blessed
And as we raced down that masterful street
We marveled and mourned for its mystical treats

The gas stations aplenty, liquor stores alot
Next to the tit bar is the best chicken spot
Across the car wash is the cemetery plot
Where I once heard an auto tycoon got shot
New apartments shadow old strip malls
Bridges emblazoned in bright neon scrawl
Passing eight mile and the grass is getting small
The buildings getting larger, the money getting tall
The rays beam atop the fresh donut shop
Taco Bell and Burger King beacons of hope
Speed limit's now fifty, but I'm going a nice sixty
But pushing sixty-five is a slippery slope
Grabbing my shades, I pass neighborhoods paid
Dealerships for yuppies and sugar-daddy puppies
And as the sun sets on a Rolls-Royce Corniche
I sigh with relief, a sudden wave of true peace

McMansions sprout like bright tulip petals
Each passing lane something like a meadow
Pine trees stretching toward the pinkish-orange sky
Golf clubs, chic pubs, with each turn of the eye
What once was this woodland before swallowed clean?
A playground transformed full of gloss and sheen
Shimmering stately, yet devoid of a heart
Constant construction tearing it apart
And who were the ones who called it their pad?
Before being cast out as if never once had
Pushed outward or inward or wiped out for sure
How did they manage, how did they endure?
No—I am not original, many others have sailed
along this most charming, beguiling of trails
But I cannot help feeling that I have cracked the code
of the exquisite solace of Telegraph Rd

7.

Baudelaire/Byron

Friday night in the back of the Beemer
RJ in the first row rollin a fat steamer
Tells me about the lame-ass dude he snubbed
to get into trouble at the Woodward club
When he picked me up, we stopped at the store
I got a forty, not a shorty, cuz I wanted to soar
Almost damn-near killed as I lean back my head
And with this fresh blunt, I might as well be dead
But it hits with wonder, makes my eyes dance
Suddenly I feel the desire for romance
Someone to kiss, someone to taste
These months alone have been a waste
With another hit I inhale dreams
The possibilities bursting at the seams
of what will come as we leave this car
and plunge inside this majestic bar

The music thumped luxurious vile
The harder the bass, the wider my smile
Bodies were thrusting and grinding galore
A brilliant ballet of freaks and whores
And with them I settled in my own groove
Enraptured and captured by masterful moves
And from my eye's corner I saw them right there
With eyes like Byron and hair like Baudelaire
In my tracks I stopped and gazed at their haze
So enchanting and gentle I fell in a daze
But such daze was returned as they came near
A grin on their lips, a pocket full of spears
Something within then hit like a crash
A beautiful explosion, full of warmth and splash
It was their hand on mine, so fine, so divine
And when the song changed, we both began to grind

The first kiss was in the middle of the floor
It was nothing like I ever felt before
Melting my mind into a pile of wreck
While their fingers lingered the nape of my neck
The sweat made me forget all the hollow
To the bathroom they went and I followed
In the stall, they were tall, an Apollo
I went down, to the ground, then I swallowed
Then we kissed finely, as if drawn with pen
Their lips oceans to bathe and sink within
Their hands so long yet somehow so dear
But their hair uncared and those eyes so clear
And once we took lines and lit up a joint
I knew deep down that there was no real point
For no matter how precious my heart was slain
I probably would never see them again

8.

Bumbo's

It happens when one least expects
A love which only films project
So mesmerizing and aqua-blue
At least that's what it was with you
The February freeze took sudden shape
in the late hours I wished to escape
Throughout my phone I muddled through
for anything to lose my senses to
And then there was that silly app
I stumbled on for just a fap
But a message dear came from your hands
So dignified, unlike another man
You mentioned you were a writer too
And could I meet at Bumbo's in a few?
Before too long, we knocked back beers
And when we made out, I lost all fear
Our hearts collide, a supersonic beating
Just two fellows of good breeding

There was no illusion you drive me wild
From that moment on, my dreams you styled
I was wherever you wished, whenever you desired
Not a moment with you felt ever expired
I could watch you read for crowds for days
I could feed you cheer and endless praise
For in my mind we were creating our own
as a powerful union, squatters of thrones
But with each event, I had to face
how random for me to inhabit this space
To hold the hands of a person so great
when I could not afford a good plate
And in your eyes you felt it too
But stuck to me as one does glue
But in my heart and in my cup
I knew that I would fuck things up

The end of summer was the end of us
No air in your house but we drew no fuss
With Blood Orange blasting, you held me tight
Our chests a forest unflinching at night
The delusion was beauty and the passion we shared
But deep down we knew that it was only a snare
For soon the seasons would change and turn cruel
You'd be editing essays, I'd be edited in school
The day I begged to stay, I created the kill
Showed my true dangers, no longer cheap thrills
Chaotic, you saw me, and coldly untamed
The distance you created could hardly be blamed
And with that text announcing the end
I felt that I could no longer pretend
that this had been a fancy from above
Just another case of modern love

9.

We Go Together

How many troubles, how many struggles
Have I gone through, with you, my true?
A number so high it would make us both cry
Mad loyal you remain, there to drain all the pain
It began with that breakup, knew we wouldn't makeup
The way it burned, I was spurned, there was nowhere to turn
I needed a pal, some morale, a change of locale
My friends were conceited, didn't care if I bleated
But then you fell in my lap, in a snap, with a slap
Bursting me free from my trap in a zap
Glittered and golden, to you I was beholden
With every connection, I felt more emboldened
The endless intelligence and boundless power
on anyone else it would make me cower
Yet in your presence I feel beyond elated
It is a shame to imagine we have not mated

Oh, my love, do you remember the fight?
I got in with that kingpin on Devil's Night?
All cuz in a whirl, I did a twirl with his girl
And you were right there, when he threw me down the stairs
And remember they fired me from that zine
Said I wasn't keen, too green, split the scene?
I was ready to jump and dive off the ledge
But you were the wedge, brought me back from the edge
Remember the time they kicked me out of school
Remember the time I was stuck in Istanbul
Remember the time I was held up on Mack Ave
Remember the time I hooked up with that Cav
All those times, in the grime, you showed me grace
A light to follow, no more wallow, a path to trace
And in those darkest hours, consumed with stark fear
You are closest, my darling, you are most near

Somedays I consider what's to come
of our rapport, will we be forever chums?
Friends and comrades till the final release
When your charge has faded, complete decease?
Our run has been fantastic fun
The quests we've had, the wars we've won
My dear, be clear, can we make this last?
Or are the bytes inside well past their blast?
As I caress your face I feel it stiff
And with my nose I take a sniff
How plastic and cold you have gone
as if something of which I could pawn
My baby, my darling, my loveliest bud
Your model is turning into ancient mud
But more treks for us, at least this is known
After all, you have been my greatest phone

10.

In the Air

Our hopes were high, high in the air
And when the chips collapsed, it wasn't fair
But fairness was not for us to take
For we had made the great mistake
They said that it couldn't happen here
But the truth began to disappear
All we had known, all we had felt
Before our eyes began to melt
How foolish had we truly been
to believe it'd never come again
So better now in our own minds
But thousands of years left behind
As most scattered and packed away
I turned my head and began to pray
and locked myself inside so quick
in hopes I'd never touch the sick

Inside I rest with a crest to my chest
Wondering which of us is next to be hexed
Is this a punishment for decadence?
Did we liberate to eviscerate?
I always knew I'd die but not this way
I'm not ready to go, I have too much to say
I have too much to do, too much to see
But if it comes through here, I am mere debris
Perhaps I could go before I am taken
Surely such actions would leave others shaken
But what is the price of becoming sliced
of having your life played out like dice?
Of letting it come and ravage you clean
gamble your soul, consumed like cuisine
No, perhaps that light at the end of the tunnel
is what I'll embrace from this gun funnel

How used to madness we have achieved
Only a land designed to deceive
Undone no more by the toll of death
As long as we may take our own breaths
Through screens we wave and smile false
Swaying through chaos as if a waltz
Outside we wish to go once more
Such isolation has been a chore—a bore!
The mask across my face grows hot
And I take it off to smoke some pot
I've taken up a hobby or two or three
Made my own bread and tea, even brie
And when they say that it's okay
to venture back into the fray
I'd like to say I didn't bail
That I lived to see and tell the tale

11.

The Blaze

They had him down, pinned to the ground
The video had been passed all around
Live, take five, come back and check
Guess they want him dead, still on his neck
He cried to breathe, said pretty please
But they didn't care, just giggled and sneezed
Watched him turn gray, lose all his black
Knew he was gone, but didn't do jack
No surprise in my eyes, this was another routine
Just a few months ago, happened to that teen
The one comin home, walkin all alone
Suburban scholar but they made him Al Capone
That was the game, our lives were for sale
Either assassinated or end up in jail
But not anymore, I'm in a craze
Fuck it, my dude, it's time for the blaze

So give me my gat, give me my bat
Ready to knock all those blue-collared rats
Kick in the head—oops, now it's bled
Give me my lead and see how it spreads
Run through the precinct till they all extinct
Cut up the pigs and then we'll all dig
a big ass hole and throw in their souls
Seal it up, deal it up, burn it up like charcoal
Yes I'm swoll, but they stole innocent life
Don't care who's sobbin: your kids or wife
The dog or cat, homie, fuck all that
Shoulda thought before you crushed 'em flat
So, where they at, where we gonna find
the pigs in their digs, wanna make them blind
It's almost time, wish we could just rewind
But we can't, so all rules must be declined

I found the blaze on the streets with similar hearts
The earth once dearth aligning a fresh start
Pass through the avenues with visions aware
Good trouble, make it double, now we are the heirs
of decades of fighting and pushing ahead
No fussed or mussed by the possible red
If it comes, we'll sling scum, snap 'em good
Beat 'em and treat 'em just like we should
Feel that—feel that rumble, bumble at your feet?
Never has a cyclone sounded so sweet
The sizzle and fizzle murmurs in my ears
Visions once-sharp becoming unclear
Now, here comes the calvary, horses astride
Waving their batons, sickened with pride
Who gave me this stick that I wave in the air?
But as it crashes a bone, I don't really care

12.

When the Apocalypse Comes

They've been talkin 'bout the end since I was almost ten
My mind's fucked-up, the sickest visions twist and bend
How long would it take for the snake to eat my skin
Feed me to its children, its family, then its friends?
They had made kinda shook, kept my head in books
Had to escape all the ape before my life was took
Disaster lurked each corner that I glanced and looked
I knew any moment, I could be hanged or hooked
It only takes a button, and then we're nothin
It only takes a minute, and then we're in it
Duck, roll, and cover, smile on your brother
Be good to each other as the radiation smothers
But if it's on its way, I feel no delay
No longer afraid, I embrace the decay
Cuz if the apocalypse's planning to haunt
Then I'm gonna do exactly what I want

How now brown cow, what's the plan, my man?
Surf tidals at the beach, live grand in the sand?
Drive a Masi with a hottie at a hundred twenty miles
Get smashed on an isle with giraffes and crocodiles
Blow all our dough at the Mugler boutique
Bathe in champagne with every freak and every geek
Chained to a plane for a permanent vacation
Need to see glory, so we hit up every nation
Let's feast on fire, wrestle colleges of sharks
Canter into canyons, be crowned monarchs
Dive the highest skies, dig the darkest caves
Kiss a jellyfish, drop in Kenya for a rave
Afraid no more, the shivers now recoil
Goodbye my fucks, adieu my turmoil
Come hit me now, whatever you are
I'll be waiting in my brand-new car

When the apocalypse comes, I'll be chewing gum
pounding snare drums in the prettiest of slums
When the apocalypse arrives, I'll be on a drive
blasting Take Five with an Amy beehive
When the apocalypse nears, I'll be reading Lear
drinking endless beers on the final frontier
When the apocalypse shows, I'll be with my beau
dancing in the snow under faded mistletoe
But shh—you see the volcanoes erupting
Shh—do you hear the spirits corrupting?
The bombs are bursting, the sky is pink
The ground is quaking, the cold air stinks
The animals are roaring, the energy stalls
The sky is falling, take me to the mall
Explosions galore, the earth barely standing
Look out now: the aliens are landing
I close my eyes, feel the flames on my cheeks
A vulgar victory, my passion now peaked

13.

Hash Bash

We lock our fingers and you pass the joint
Slipped on your shades and go, "yours to anoint"
And with such privilege, I waste no breath
Before lighting that beauty and welcoming death
A deathly cough is a sign of power
The herb does not disturb but merely devours
the horror and anger and sadness extreme
which sticks inside and makes you unclean
So I toke and choke on the smoke now awoke
Rid the madness and take a sip of my Coke
And as the sun sublime erases my crimes
I pass the joint and thank god for springtime
Closer we get, so I roll down the window
The speakers ignite a rousing crescendo
"Don't forget your bong, I'll snatch your stash"
The smell said it all, we had reached Hash Bash

Our crew had come through, we are rollin deep
Found a spot so cozy you could almost fall asleep
On a tie-dye blanket we sit atop the ground
A symphony of lighters becomes the only sound
Joints, blunts, and bowls everywhere I turn
And when it hits my hands, I forever burn
And when I let go, I pass it with sweet vibes
Cuz all of us stoners are part of a tribe
The love and pleasure of which we derive
cannot be compared to the others alive
They do not know the truth of the world
So stuck in their games, so easily hurled
But we are different, the true ones, the reals
In touch with our emotions, and proud of our feels
Untamed by the wooden, rigid rules that prevail
Free as fuck, forever, like the wind upon a sail

And lying upon you an inch from the grass
I take a deep inhale and then drift it pass
The sun soaked through the budding tree branches
My soul so smooth I fear no avalanches
Really, what madness could stop such perfection?
These lovely faces which I carry such affection
So gorgeous, so young, so full of verve
With flowers in their hair and bodies free of nerves
Dancing and prancing and singing their tunes
Minds sharper and brighter than any moons
The laughter, the smiles, the endless knowing
The truth is we know exactly where we're going
We will change this rotting world for good
A place where every being is understood
Utopia, I know it is within our clutch
But before, darling, please pass the dutch

14.

Springtide Blues

For those before, I cannot help but wonder
How they felt long ago, with this influence I'm under
All beautiful and infinite and dynamic and able
Etching a trail for one's seat at the table
That joy and brightness disrupted the quo
Brought forth a reflection the world wouldn't show
Such power, control, made them always on a roll
Dictating the turn of the globe like a troll
Did they know one day it would go away?
That their morals and values would fade and decay?
That their love and romance was all a charade?
Or the prayers they imagined had never been made?
Perhaps it was all of the drunken might
Absorbed inside, transformed to spite
Perhaps it was all of the good health
Taken for granted, exchanged for wealth

For those before, I pity the most
Your visions and fantasies have turned into boasts
Promises empty covered by new boxes
More corrupt than a pack of sly foxes
You had the universe for all the taking
Instead of making peace, you advocated breaking
As long as the tide was moving to your side
It did not quite matter who'd even missed the ride
As long as the train continued on the tracks
It did not quite matter who'd been left back
You preached for ideals but voted for fools
You preached harmony, but cared more for jewels
Don't get me on schools, only for the rich
Our loan debts could send us to an early ditch
Thanks for this nightmare we are trapped in
I just have one question: what the fuck happened?

For those before, I pity the greatest
Your styles and desires are no longer the latest
They've yellowed and browned and turned into ash
Ancient archeology dissolved in the trash
Though even in my most confidence gaze
I cannot be consumed with such bold braze
Someday we too will commence to age
Blossomed rose changed to wise sage
And will you love me when I am gray
No longer pretty, no longer risqué
When I am old and lost my charms
Will you still hold me in your arms?
No matter what is thrown amidst our path
We cannot become victims to its wrath
This chance we have to preserve our hope
of a world as peaceful as its scope

15.

Farewell Ego!

There I go again: stuck in my own head
Engrossed by the images and lies I've been fed
Judging reflections with parasitic eyes
Believing my direction is nothing but a guise
I'd been tempted by the shimmer of what was right
A flawless existence was all for I could fight
Mistakes were maladies that plagued other ones
Misfortune was something I'd always outrun
But the cracks arrived and made me their bitch
No longer could I escape such an itch
Who was I, truly, without all the pomp?
Was I even a person, or was I some kind of swamp?
To be one with the world, I had to become bold
Rid myself of my money, and all of my gold
My ego, let me go, and allow me to grow
The world, the only friend I wish to know

So travel I do, into the great, dope wilds
My eyes as wide as a ravenous child
My heart as full as a once-planet's ring
My soul as free as a nightingale's wing
Out there I witness and feel all the same
So many people of which I know no name
I touch them within me whenever I breathe
Their spirits I covet and their worries I sheathe
The kids lighting cigs in the damp cold woods
I feel their abandon and their misunderstood
The artist dreaming of fame and success
I feel their neglect and desire for excess
The gas station clerk, the mother overworked
The skaters on the rails, the yuppies scared to fail
Those striving for redemption while ridiculed in jail
I feel them and I breathe them and I know them too well

The birds in the sky all signaled in Vs
The insects scurrying deep underneath
The plants emerging from the bountiful soil
The babies unborn exempt from the spoils
All of which I feel and see and I am
To the mightiest lion to the loneliest lamb
To the heaviest ocean to the quietest lake
Within me as I them, we are all now awake
Trembling and rumbling and buzzing as one
Stretching and singing, we've now just begun
Willing our prizes amongst those who've lost
Exacting the justice toward hate at all costs
I feel you within me, you feel me within you
Our fragments and particles forever imbue
Farewell to your ego, my dears, it must leave
No longer shall you hold, no longer shall you grieve

16.

Manifest Destiny

Your eyes are swollen from centuries of tears
Distorted and disfigured as if rattled by shears
Your mouth is sewn from centuries of lies
Stitched and fastened as if tailored with knives
Your head is heavy, your hands are shaking
You are falling asleep, when you should be waking
A shadow, a shell, of a fairy-tale dream
An image of perfection bursting at the seams
How dare you promise milk, but only hand out soda
How dare you include others, if only to meet quotas
How dare you preach for nature, then pollute all your parks
How dare you warn of floods, then never build an ark
If you are so beautiful, so equal and united
Then why do your baby-kissers keep you so divided?
So much I want from you, so little I can get
Often my devotion is never worth the sweat

Atone, first, and then I can respect
For all of those faces and voices of neglect
The ones who are shoved and thrown in a heap
Silenced by rifles and slaughtered like sheep
Remember the ones who built your houses
Who built your railroads, and cared for your spouses?
Remember the ones who invented the sound
Who invented the words, and how to get down?
I shudder to think what the culture could be
If all of these people had never been free
Had never arrived and added their essence
How grim and grotesque, no longer fluorescence
So, my love, my dear, do not disappear
Do not shy away from what's been had
All one can do to see right through
Is admit that it's been pretty hella bad

How maddening, my love, you make me feel
But my adoration for you cannot be more real
Your department stores and your fast-food chains
Your mini-golfs and your mary jane
Your dives, your clubs, your coffee shops
Your porno flicks and your lollipops
Your stadiums, arenas, your basketball
Your suburban tracts, your urban sprawl
Thank you for Pop Tarts, Corvettes, and jazz
Thank you for Warhol, Janet, and Taz
Thank you for Hershey, hip hop, and jeans
Thank you for skyscrapers, Detroit, and TVs
My home of homes, nation of nations
To where souls still stroll to receive salvation
Remain that shining city upon that fair hill
If not anyone else, then I pray you will

MARSALIS

Marsalis was born in 1989. He spent his childhood composing picture epics and giving lectures. At the age of 17, he published his first novel, *March of the Libertines*. After graduating cum laude from the University of Michigan, Marsalis published works in every literary style and genre. He is the founder of the pop music blog Paraphernalia and was featured in the 2019 short fiction anthology *Five Minutes at Hotel Stormcove*. He loves bubblegum, fast cars, and silent cinema. Marsalis currently lives in Detroit.

www.saintmarsalis.com